BEFORE THE BATTLE:

Choosing Peace Through Pre-Suit Mediation

A guide for Florida couples who want clarity, control, and closure – without going to war

Supreme Ct. Certified Mediator

Attorney Beth Reineke

Jacobs & Whitehall

9600 Escarpment Blvd

Suite 745-282

Austin, TX 78749

www.jacobsandwhitehall.com

Ordering Information:

Quantity sales. Special discounts are available on quantity purchases by corporations, associations, and others. For details, contact the publisher at the address above.

Orders by U.S. trade bookstores and wholesalers. Please contact Jacobs & Whitehall: Tel: (888) 570-7338 or visit www.jacobsandwhitehall.com.

Printed in the United States of America

Published in 2025

TABLE OF CONTENTS

PREFACE

Who This Book Is For

This book is for anyone facing divorce who wants to avoid the stress, expense, and drawn-out ordeal of a court battle. You may have heard of mediation but still feel unsure about what the process really involves or whether it could work for you.

My goal with this guide is to give you the clarity and confidence to consider Pre-Suit Divorce Mediation before you hire a divorce lawyer, before you turn to AI, and before you rely on a DIY generic online form. When you understand your options, you can make decisions from a place of knowledge—not fear.

Divorce does not have to destroy you financially, emotionally, or personally. Pre-Suit Mediation offers a path forward that is often faster, less stressful, and more predictable. Most importantly, it allows you to move into the next chapter of your life with greater stability and a stronger foundation.

DISCLAIMER

This publication is intended to be used for educational purposes only. No legal advice is being given, and no attorney-client relationship is intended to be created by reading this material. The author assumes no liability for any errors or omissions or for how this book or its contents are used or interpreted, or for any consequences resulting directly or indirectly from the use of this book. For legal or any other advice, please consult an experienced attorney or the appropriate expert, who is aware of the specific facts of your case and is knowledgeable in the law in your jurisdiction.

Reineke Mediations
4950 West Kennedy Blvd.
Suite 302
Tampa, FL 33609
www.bethreineke.com
(813) 205-6675

Testimonials

"I can't thank Beth Reineke enough for making what could have been a stressful and emotional process so simple and straightforward. From the very beginning, she was clear, efficient, and incredibly easy to work with. She handled everything quickly, communicated every step of the way, and made sure I felt supported throughout the entire process. If you're looking for an amazing lawyer who knows exactly what they're doing and can help you get through a divorce with minimal stress and maximum efficiency, I highly recommend Beth G. Reineke. She truly made a difficult time feel manageable and fast! Thank you!"

– Lisa

******

"I absolutely recommend Beth Reineke for your service. Highly professional and knowledgeable at a fair price. These things are never easy to go through, however hiring Beth made the whole process seamless. Thank you!"

– Kimberly

******

"Working with Beth was a straightforward and seamless process. She was very kind, professional and there were no hidden costs. She presented all of our options, the cost, and provided detailed instructions on how the process would go. We were able to complete our documents in two sessions. Once we completed all documents, Beth organized the documents into folders, with instructions on what to do with all the documents. The court was satisfied with all our documents and our divorce was completed without any additional documents needed by the courts."

– Rochelle

******

"Beth Reineke has mediated several of my dissolution of marriage cases and helped settle some that I never thought would actually settle. She does a really good job of helping you evaluate your position and weigh the pros and cons of it so your clients can make meaningful decisions. I highly recommend her as a mediator for family law cases."

– Atty. Kay

******

Attorney Mediator Beth Reineke : My Background

I graduated with honors from the University of South Florida with a degree in finance, then went on to earn my law degree from the University of Florida. After graduating, I joined a mid-sized commercial law firm, where I spent the first several years of my career handling a wide range of commercial cases. My work included drafting and litigating contracts, collection actions, foreclosures, commercial disputes, commercial landlord-tenant matters, employment law, and probate and guardianship cases. And, although the firm did not commonly practice family law, from time to time, I handled divorce cases for my commercial clients.

In 1993, I opened my own firm. As the years went on, the number of my family law cases steadily grew until they became the center of my practice. By 1997, I fully embraced the path I was on, phasing out my other case types and devoting myself to family law. That same year, I received my Supreme Court Certification as a marital and family law mediator.

In 2000, I took on one of the most challenging professional steps any attorney can take. I applied to become Board Certified. The process is highly selective. Only a small handful of attorneys each year meet the requirements to sit for the Board Certification Exam. The Family Law Exam has less than a 50% pass rate. The year I took the exam, about 20 attorneys statewide qualified to take the exam, but only 2 of us passed the exam going on to become Board Certified Marital and Family Lawyers. At the time, there were only 270 Board Certified Divorce Attorneys statewide; 22, including myself, were in the Tampa Bay Area.

My work extended beyond the courtroom as well. After Certification, I became more active in the family bar association. I served on the Executive Council for the Family Law Section of the Hillsborough County Bar Association. I was president for a couple of years of a local collaborative divorce organization. I was one of the instructors for the National Business Institute (NBI), teaching family law to other attorneys. I volunteered at the Centre for Women in Tampa, where I taught a monthly class to individuals on Florida divorce law. I also published several articles on family law issues in state and local Bar Journals, continuing to share my hard earned knowledge with my colleagues.

How I Came To Focus On Mediation, Not Litigation

Towards the end of my litigation practice, because of my growing reputation as a litigator, all I was doing was representing clients in hotly contested cases. No one talks about the cases you settle; they talk about the cases you've litigated and won; as if you can actually win a family law case. In my opinion, "You don't WIN a contested divorce case, as a client you survive it." There are just too many downsides to litigating.

The best cases and the happiest clients were my clients who settled their cases out of court. After litigating for years, I finally decided that there had to be a better way; and that better way is Pre-Suit Divorce Mediation.

Introduction: When You Know It's Time To Choose A Different Path

Mediation Reduces Stress And Puts You Back In Control

Many people don't realize that divorce doesn't have to start with lawyers filing papers, spouses being served, and a case unfolding in court. You do have a choice in how your divorce is handled.

Pre-Suit Divorce Mediation allows you and your spouse to sit down together with the help of a neutral mediator and work through the issues yourselves.

Instead of a judge making the decisions for your family, you stay in control. You decide how to divide your assets and debts. You decide what arrangement is best for your children. You decide if support is paid, and if so, how much and for how long.

That freedom to decide for yourself can make all the difference. The best part? Mediation doesn't just save time and money. It spares you much of the stress and upheaval that comes with a lawsuit. For many families, it's the path that offers not only resolution but also peace of mind.

When you are ready to discuss whether Pre-suit Divorce Mediation is right for you, contact us at **Reineke Mediations** (813) 205-6675.

PART I:

WHY THE SYSTEM IS BROKEN & WHAT MOST PEOPLE GET WRONG

CHAPTER 1:
DIVORCE DOESN'T HAVE TO BE A WAR

Misunderstandings About Florida Divorce Court

If you are like most people, you may believe that if you hire an attorney and litigate you are going to have your "day in court". You believe that you will get to tell your story to a sympathetic, open-minded judge; be heard and be able to share your side of events.

Unfortunately, the harsh reality is that this is not how divorce court works. In reality, you will have to sit through the majority of your trial and speak only when spoken to, answering only questions that are deemed relevant by the court.

What is relevant to the court is not *why* you are getting a divorce or *how* you've been wronged. What is relevant to a court is whether you have minor or dependent children and what are your "Marital" assets and liabilities.

Furthermore, while the best interest of the children is still the benchmark. This standard is narrowed by the statutory presumption in Florida that 50/50 timesharing (also known as visitation) is best for every child (sometimes despite the circumstances).

Additionally, while Florida is an "Equitable Distribution" state, the court rarely deviates from a 50/50 distribution of a couples' Marital Assets and Marital Liabilities. The court doesn't take a chainsaw to every asset and debt, but the parties' net worths (assets minus debts) post-divorce will likely be equal.

What happens if you don't like the judge's decisions? Florida family law judges have enormous discretion with regard to asset and liability division and visitation. Appeals of a trial judge's rulings are expensive and almost impossible to win.

The Unseen Expenses Of Divorce Litigation

Apart from uncertainty, divorce litigation is alarmingly expensive. And, when you hire a divorce attorney, 8-12 months later, you'll be in court-ordered mediation, discussing the very issues you could have resolved months ago for a fraction of the cost, using Pre-Suit Divorce Mediation.

Let's look at the numbers. In litigation, a $5,000 retainer doesn't go very far. You're charged for every pleading, every phone call, every email, every text, every photocopy, every postage stamp, and any other expense the law firm can pass on to you.

When you retain an attorney at the onset of your divorce case, the attorney is likely not going to be focused on settling your case. They're focused on putting out fires and on the deadlines presented by the court's mandatory financial disclosure requirements. What delays matters even more is that many attorneys don't review financial records themselves. Very few have a financial background like I do. Instead, they hire a forensic CPA to review the records and report back to them, and this expert's fees become another expense that is passed on to you.

When the documents are finally received and reviewed, the attorney may decide depositions (formal questioning of the parties and potential witnesses on the record) are required prior to developing settlement options. A further delay and expense.

Typically, after formal discovery is completed to the attorneys' satisfaction, the parties will then attend mandatory court-ordered mediation, where about 80% of cases settle. If your attorney has not done much work on your case, you may have only spent around $25,000 over the 6-8+ months that the attorney has been representing you. However, if there were temporary relief issues (such as motions for support, visitation, exclusive possession of the home or to stop the dissipation of assets), you have likely spent your hard earned $25,000 in the first 60 days of your case. By the time you get to court-ordered mediation, you have probably spent two to three times that amount. And, if your case doesn't settle, the sky is the limit.

In other words, litigation is a bottomless well. Your attorney will do their job, but it will likely cost you a small fortune. And, if at any point you cannot pay your monthly bill or an additional retainer, all work stops, and the attorney will ask the court to withdraw as counsel, leaving you with no representation whatsoever.

What does Pre-Suit Divorce Mediation offer in contrast? When you work with me, you are also charged hourly for my time, but it is time spent primarily with you in mediation.

Mediation sessions are broken up into two-hour blocks of time, and many couples settle in their very first session. You pay for each mediation session as you move through the process. A retainer is only paid once a settlement has been reached. And, this is a set amount to cover the time I spend drafting your contract(s) and court documents. It's a far simpler, more predictable, and more cost-effective path forward that saves you not only time and money but stress, as well, when compared to both parties hiring two competing attorneys and filing for divorce.

The Emotional Impacts Of Litigation

Emotionally, litigation tends to maximize conflict. The emotional turmoil suffered during a divorce can be crushing; I've seen clients descend into intense and lasting depressions and even become suicidal during especially difficult, drawn-out divorce cases.

Another consideration is that court hearings position you and your spouse as adversaries, often prolonging bitterness and further damaging co-parenting relationships. This adversarial process can be especially hard on children, who may feel caught in the middle of ongoing disputes.

Additionally, court actions often require you to air extremely personal information, adding to stress and reducing privacy. In court, judges, not you or your spouse, ultimately control the final outcome, which can leave you feeling powerless and dissatisfied with court-imposed solutions.

Mediation is different. Pre-Suit Divorce Mediation fosters communication, privacy, and creative problem-solving. This allows you and your spouse to craft tailored agreements that honor your family's unique needs, lessen emotional distress, and greatly reduce long-term harm to your family's relationships.

CHAPTER 2:
WHAT PRE-SUIT MEDIATION IS & WHY IT MATTERS

The Basics Of Pre-Suit Mediation

During pre-suit mediation, you and your spouse will meet with the mediator together. The mediator will act as a neutral facilitator and gatekeeper, keeping your conversations about your divorce courteous and productive. The various aspects of your divorce, such as asset and debt distribution, timesharing, alimony, and child support will be discussed rather than fought for. If financial records need to be reviewed, they are contractually required to be provided voluntarily.

Because I have a background in finance and have been working as an attorney for over 30 years, when you work with me, the majority of the time, we will not need the assistance of a financial expert. Instead, I can assist you and your spouse in reviewing your financial records, organizing them, and talking you through the pros and cons of various financial settlements.

If both of you are committed to reaching a settlement, you will settle and can then file for an uncontested divorce. You'll be done much quicker and will have spent a small fraction of what you would have spent had you both hired competing attorneys.

When Is Pre-Suit Mediation Right For You?

Knowing when to start the pre-suit mediation can help set a productive tone for your divorce. Here are some signs that it may be time to consider mediation:

Communication: Pre-Suit Divorce Mediation works best if both spouses are willing to at least try to communicate in a respectful manner. Pre-suit mediation requires both spouses to be willing to discuss their needs and concerns openly. Your mediator, as your facilitator, will keep discussions respectful, productive, and on topic. Even if there are areas of disagreement, as long as both parties are willing to listen as well as talk, mediation can be an effective solution.

Proactive: Mediation is a proactive step for those who are prepared to move forward with their divorce but wish to do so outside of the courtroom. If you agree about ending the marriage but haven't officially filed for divorce, starting mediation early can create a more harmonious exit strategy.

Timely: Florida's court dockets can be crowded, meaning a contested divorce can drag on for months or even years. If you're hoping to avoid a drawn-out legal battle, beginning pre-suit mediation early can fast-track your divorce, allowing you to address all key issues early on and move toward closure more swiftly.

Confidential: The confidential nature of mediation is often a factor that couples find significant. If you're concerned about maintaining confidentiality regarding finances, family dynamics, or business interests, early pre-suit mediation allows you to work out agreements in a secure, private environment, away from public court records, hearings and trial.

Finally, and most importantly for families with minor children, pre-suit mediation allows you to create a customized detailed parenting plan that addresses custody, visitation, and shared parenting arrangements. When both parents prioritize their children's well-being, mediation can help establish a cooperative co-parenting relationship and reduce the impact of the divorce on the family. Remember, a judge may or may not hand down a custody order that works well for you and your family. And no judge can fully understand or appreciate the background of your marriage, family dynamics, or relationships with your children as well as with your spouse.

When Pre-Suit Mediation Is Not Your Best Option

You will want to consider consulting with and possibly retaining an independent family lawyer if your divorce case involves domestic violence, parental kidnapping, a significant dissipation of your marital assets, being cut off from your financial resources, or drug or alcohol abuse problems that significantly impact parenting abilities.

I can still mediate complex divorces that involve the above issues, but if you or your children's safety is a concern, representation prior to and during mediation may be in order.

Common Misconceptions About Divorce Mediation

If I mediate without an attorney, I am going to get steamrolled by my spouse. This is simply not the case. As your mediator, I am neutral, and I don't take sides. However, I am also the gatekeeper. It is my job to ensure that both parties have the opportunity to meaningfully participate in the process and that each party has the information they need to make informed decisions about their future.

If I choose Pre-Suit Divorce Mediation, then I can't talk to a family lawyer if I have a question. This couldn't be farther from the truth. I often suggest to parties that they confer with an attorney prior to coming to mediation, so that they will have a general understanding about what their rights and obligations are under Florida law. Additionally, because mediation sessions are broken up into two-hour blocks of time and there is often a lag between a verbal agreement and a written agreement, there is ample time to confer with an attorney between mediation sessions. Finally, I encourage all of my clients to have the draft agreements (contracts) reviewed by an attorney if they don't understand them or have any remaining questions that I have not been able to answer.

I won't understand the agreement if an attorney doesn't explain it to me. First, you should always remember that, as your mediator, I am neutral; I am not looking to put something into your agreement that you did not agree to or leave something out of your agreement that you did agree to. And, one of my primary goals is to write contracts that are easily understandable. In my opinion, if you and your spouse understand what you are agreeing to and are comfortable with it, you are less likely to fight about it later. I want you to stay out of court now and in the future.

PART II:

What Peaceful Divorce Looks Like

CHAPTER 3:
MEDIATION 101

What Mediation Is

Mediation is a way for you and the other party to regain control of your divorce. It's a way for me to help both of you understand your options, your court's requirements, and work together towards a settlement agreement that you both can live with.

The process can and will save you time, money, stress, and future litigation if you are both willing to work together; communicating and negotiating in good faith.

What Mediation Is Not

To be clear, mediation is not marriage counseling. Many clients, especially those who are not yet ready on an emotional level to admit that the marriage is ending, tend to think of mediation as a form of counseling or therapy.

Your mediator is not your therapist. I am not here to listen to you and your spouse yell at one another, nor am I here to fix your marriage. I am also not here to encourage you to get divorced; that decision is for the two of you to make independently.

If you truly can't communicate, with some assistance, or if one or both of you is facing intense anger issues, it would be best for each of you to hire separate attorneys and return to my mediation table with attorney representation.

Mediation exists to empower you and help you understand the avenues available for settlement. Finally, the mediation process lets the two of you work toward a divorce that is far more secure, fair, and legally solid than a divorce attempted alone, without input, or without the right guidance. An Attorney/Mediator can provide the guidance you need to reach a fair result.

CHAPTER 4:
WHAT TO EXPECT IN THE MEDIATION PROCESS

Making The Call

If you are considering mediation in the Tampa Bay area, please reach out to **Reineke Mediations** for a free telephone consultation. I serve clients throughout the Tampa Bay Area and the State of Florida. If you live outside of the Tampa Bay Area, we can schedule virtual mediation sessions and work with each other remotely.

Have questions about Pre-Suit Divorce Mediation, but unsure if the process is right for you? Call me at **(813) 205-6675;** or email me at **beth@bethreineke.com**.

Our initial telephone call will help determine if pre-suit mediation is a good fit for you and for your spouse. I can also answer any specific questions you may have about pre-suit mediation or mediation as a whole.

How I Approach Pre-Suit Mediation

My pre-suit divorce mediations are scheduled in two-hour blocks of time. This allows us to accomplish much more in less time compared to traditional mediations where attorneys and clients sit in separate rooms for half-day or full-day sessions. All the while the attorneys' meters are running. My structure keeps the process focused, efficient, and cost effective.

As the mediator, I remain neutral. I do not take sides, and I cannot provide either party with legal advice. What I can do is educate both spouses about Florida's statutes and black-letter irrefutable law while offering practical insights to help them evaluate their options.

I also work closely with the parties to develop settlement proposals, weigh the pros and cons of each option, and create tools that help them visualize the outcomes. For example, I prepare financial schedules so couples can see the real impact of various settlement choices, and I draft timesharing charts to help parents evaluate whether a proposed schedule will work for them and their children. I also calculate child support and guide parties through discussions about alimony.

Once a settlement is reached, I take a retainer based upon the time necessary to prepare your contracts and all the court documents required by your county for an uncontested divorce. This includes both the Marital Settlement Agreement and a Parenting Plan, when children are involved. Unlike some mediators who simply fill in pre-purchased forms, I draft customized contracts that reflect the family's unique circumstances.

Drafting a customized contract takes skills. Skills you learn in law school and skills you learn over years of practice, drafting, reviewing and sometimes challenging contracts. Some attorneys are better at drafting contracts than others. I started out my career drafting and litigating commercial contracts. I have drafted thousands of contracts. And, while there is no such thing as the perfect contract, I take steps all through the pre-suit mediation process to ensure that my contracts, once signed, will be valid and enforceable.

My clients have chosen their solutions, and they understand what they are agreeing to, so they are highly unlikely to fight about the terms of their agreement now or in the future. And if they do fight, they will have contracts that will guide them towards an out of court resolution, so hopefully, they don't have to hire attorneys to enforce their agreements. This helps lessen stress, conflict, and expenses for both of you now and well into the future.

When One Spouse Seems To Be Calling All The Shots

During mediation, it is not uncommon for one spouse to feel intimidated or overwhelmed while the other is more dominant in the discussions. As an experienced mediator, I manage this imbalance to ensure both of you have a voice in the process. I often slow the pace, break issues into smaller steps, and check in directly with the quieter spouse to confirm their understanding and comfort with proposed options.

If necessary, I may meet briefly with each of you separately to give the overwhelmed party space to express concerns without pressure. I also provide education about Florida law and offer practical tools—such as financial schedules or timesharing charts—so that your decisions are based on facts rather than power dynamics.

The best solutions are those that restore balance and allow both of you to participate meaningfully in the mediation process. This helps ensure any agreement reached is truly voluntary, fair, and more likely to hold up over time.

The Role Of Financial Disclosure and "The Numbers"

Florida is known as a no-fault divorce state. In general, what this means is that divorce settlements in Florida are primarily financial transactions. This makes voluntary, full and accurate financial disclosures key components of pre-suit divorce mediation. When couples mediate with me they sign a mediation contract agreeing to be transparent and to promptly provide copies of any financial records or pertinent information I request or their spouse requests.

Marital vs. Separate Assets & Liabilities

Often one party has handled the finances for the family, leaving the other party feeling in the dark when a divorce takes place. As the mediator, I believe one important role is to make sure that both spouses fully understand the nature and value of their financial assets and liabilities (debts).

Both spouses need to understand what a "Marital" Asset or Liability is and what it is not. In general, a Marital Asset or Liability is presumptively an asset or liability that was acquired during the parties' marriage.

But a "Marital assets" needs to have been acquired from a source connected with the marriage. An example of a marital asset would be earnings earned during the marriage and contributed to a savings account, or an existing 401K or IRA account.

A "Marital Liability" in general needs to have in some way benefited the family and not harmed the families' financial portfolio. Marital Liabilities often include mortgages, car loans, student loans, and credit card debt. Lack of knowledge of a liability prior to the parties' separation and impending divorce is not usually a defense.

Making Your Finances Fair and Straightforward

As the mediator, I am neutral. I don't take sides, and I cannot give either party legal advice. I can offer practical advice and educate the parties on irrefutable (usually statutory) law.

I help parties develop settlement scenarios and weigh the pros and cons of each scenario. Sometimes, I prepare financial schedules, so clients can see what their finances look like and the impact of various asset and debt distributions. I calculate child support pursuant to Florida's Child Support Guidelines and help clients understand and negotiate alimony.

When you hire me, the financial guesswork is taken out of your divorce. You and your spouse are then free to negotiate terms that are clear, well understood by both parties, and usually far more agreeable than a decision handed down by a judge.

The Benefits Of Virtual Mediation

At **Reineke Mediations**, I also offer virtual mediation sessions. When spouses separate, distance doesn't have to be the biggest problem. Sometimes spouses already live in different cities. Or one spouse may have relocated out of state, or travel schedules make it difficult to meet in person. In those cases, virtual mediation can be the ideal solution. With today's secure technology, couples can resolve their divorce from almost anywhere without setting foot in the same room or in a courtroom.

The process begins with scheduling. You'll first contact **Reineke Mediations** at **(813) 205-6675** to discuss whether your case is appropriate for Pre-Suit Divorce Mediation. Once both you and your spouse agree to move forward, we will schedule your virtual mediation session. I'll provide each of you with a secure video conferencing link (usually through Zoom) along with clear instructions for logging in.

On the day of the mediation, each spouse will join the virtual session from their own private location. Couples often appreciate that they do not have to sit side by side in the same room during discussions. Each spouse has their own screen, which can reduce tension and help both parties feel more comfortable.

As we progress, the virtual mediation session may alternate between joint discussions and private "breakout" rooms. In joint discussions, both of you are on-screen with me to share perspectives and review options.

If necessary, I'll meet separately with each of you to explore concerns more candidly and help generate solutions. The breakout room feature is one of the more effective aspects of virtual mediation. It mimics the privacy of stepping into a separate office without the stress of physically moving between spaces.

Throughout the process, the mediator helps identify common ground, clarify misunderstandings, and propose options that meet each party's goals. Pre-suit Divorce Mediation does not rush couples—it gives them time to think, ask questions, and work through issues at a pace that feels manageable. Most Florida couples who pursue pre-suit or uncontested divorce mediation settle, and then sign their agreement(s) in just four to six weeks, whether in person or virtually.

Once you and your spouse reach an understanding on all issues, I'll prepare a written agreement. This document reflects the decisions made during your virtual mediation and provides clarity for the next steps in finalizing the divorce.

The convenience of virtual mediation continues here; agreements can be reviewed, signed, and exchanged electronically, saving time and travel. Documents that must be signed in ink can simply be FedExed to you, signed, and sent back to my office.

The result? Virtual mediation with **Reineke Mediations** makes divorce and family law resolution more accessible than ever.

PART III:
AVOIDING "THE TRAP"

CHAPTER 5:
THE PERILS OF ATTEMPTING DIVORCE WITHOUT THE *RIGHT* HELP

How "Friendly" Divorces Become Unfair

Don't make the mistake of thinking your "friendly" divorce won't require any professional assistance. The reality is, an initially friendly separation can quickly become unfair, especially when one party, sometimes unbeknownst to the other party, hires their own attorney.

When one spouse has legal representation, that attorney advocates **exclusively** for their client's interests. The other spouse may feel pressured to agree to terms without fully understanding their implications. This can lead to one-sided agreements, especially in complex matters like property division, alimony, child support, or timesharing schedules.

In contrast, a neutral attorney-mediator, like me, represents neither party. I will guide both of you through the process equally. I help ensure that each person understands Florida law, and the settlement alternatives, and has the necessary information to make informed decisions. Without this neutral guidance, even amicable divorces can unintentionally favor one spouse. This often results in agreements that are financially or emotionally very unfair and potentially more difficult to modify later.

Consider a woman over 60 whose husband had his own attorney at the time of their divorce years earlier. Her husband repeatedly assured her that he would "always take care of her." Trusting his words, she signed the marital settlement agreement drafted by her husband's attorney.

The agreement made *no mention* of alimony or her entitlement to financial support. Years later, when she was ready to retire, she came to see me about alimony. Unfortunately, she discovered she had no legal basis to request alimony, over her ex-husband's current objection, because the agreement did not address alimony. In Florida, if an agreement does not at least reserve jurisdiction to award alimony at a later date, a party has effectively waived any future claim.

This example illustrates the principle, "*You don't know what you don't know.*" Even well-intentioned spouses can inadvertently give up critical rights when they lack guidance. A neutral attorney-mediator, like me, helps ensure that agreements are not one sided and accurately reflect the terms of the couples' verbal agreement. The Mediation Process, which includes drafting settlement agreements, balances knowledge and safeguards fairness, even in amicable divorces.

In short, a DIY "friendly" divorce can "unintentionally" undermine equality and fairness, whereas mediation ensures balanced, informed decision-making for both parties, and accurately drafted contracts.

Considering A DIY Forms?

When navigating divorce, custody, or other family law matters in Florida, it can be tempting to turn to online DIY forms. After all, these cookie-cutter forms are cheap, easy to download, and seem to offer a fast solution to stress. But these generic templates can come with hidden risks, and often end up costing more time, money, and emotional energy in the long run.

Here's why custom legal agreements created through mediation with a skilled attorney/mediator are not just better—they're essential.

DIY legal forms are designed to be broadly applicable across many situations. But no two families are the same. What works for one divorcing couple may be entirely unworkable for another. Financial settlements, parenting time, holiday schedules, financial support, and communication guidelines are just a few areas that need to be carefully phrased, not chosen from a dropdown menu.

For instance, generic forms often use vague language or leave critical issues unaddressed. The form you printed out may say that you and your former spouse will split parenting time "equally", without clarifying exact days, pick-up times, or school vs. summer visitation schedules.

These gaps create confusion, leading to arguments or, worse, a return to court for clarification or enforcement. Custom drafted agreements are designed to be clear, detailed, and enforceable, reducing the likelihood of disputes down the road. Conflicting or incomplete DIY form agreements often require expensive post-judgment modifications, enforcement actions, or emergency hearings. Sometimes the court can fix the problem, and sometimes it can't or won't because of the way the agreement was drafted. By contrast, investing in a well-drafted, customized agreement upfront helps you avoid costly clean-up down the road.

Finally, DIY forms don't offer professional guidance. A form can't answer your questions, help you weigh options, or think strategically about long-term consequences. It won't warn you about hidden risks, or suggest better alternatives. A skilled attorney/mediator does all this and more—empowering you to make informed, confident decisions.

I understand the unique challenges Florida families face. Through pre-suit mediation and attorney-guided document preparation, we help you create agreements that are not only legally sound but also practical, personal, and durable. Don't gamble your future on a generic cookie cutter form.

Are AI-Drafted Agreements A Good Option?

Many of my clients have begun using AI to draft what *seem* to be well-worded settlement agreements. But is this wise? Can ChatGPT handle your divorce?

In short, no, it cannot. In my experience, by far, the biggest risks of using AI to draft a marital settlement agreement or parenting plan in Florida stem from the inability of AI to *fully account* for the complexities of your unique family situation and the nuances of Florida law.

While AI can generate generic templates, it *cannot* provide personalized legal analysis, anticipate potential disputes, or ensure compliance with Florida statutes. AI cannot offer the intuitive guidance that comes from decades of experience in family law. As an attorney-mediator, I bring over 30 years of experience drafting and reviewing Marital Settlement Agreements and Parenting Plans. I draft agreements that are clear, enforceable, and tailored to each family's circumstances. I calculate child support, evaluate alimony options, prepare timesharing charts, and create financial schedules—tasks AI cannot reliably perform with accuracy or context.

Additionally, AI-generated documents may contain ambiguous language, omit critical provisions, or fail to reflect the parties' true intentions, increasing the risk of future litigation. Unlike AI, I work directly with both parties to craft agreements that are fair, practical, and legally valid; ensuring approval by the court, reducing conflict, and protecting both parents' long-term interests.

While AI may be able to present you with a general settlement agreement template, it won't factor in a truly equitable distribution. Nor can it account for your unique circumstances that may require a proper deviation from the norm. When you turn to AI for your divorce documents, you risk, if not guarantee, future litigation costs, court fees, and the emotional toll of future ongoing disputes.

I've already seen the impact. What seems like a simple, free tool brings with it future enforcement actions, emergency motions, modification petitions, and contempt proceedings. In other words, the money you seem to have "saved" with AI today becomes tomorrow's crushingly expensive legal bill.

Let's crunch some numbers. The average cost of a well-drafted mediated parenting plan ranges from $1,000 to $2,000. The cost to litigate disputes when your poorly drafted AI agreement that lands you in court could be as high as $10,000 or more per issue.

AI-generated Marital Settlement Agreements may seem convenient and affordable—but in Florida family law, mistakes in your divorce agreement can be costly, difficult to correct, and sometimes irreversible. A valid marital settlement agreement must be specific, complete, and enforceable, and should reflect your unique financial situation—not just a template.

I have over 30 years of experience helping divorcing couples resolve their financial issues through neutral, attorney-guided mediation. I ensure that every marital settlement agreement complies with Florida law and minimizes the risk of future disputes.

If you are considering divorce, choose experience over automation. Contact us to ensure your marital settlement agreement is done right the first time. Call **(813) 205-6675** or email me at **beth@bethreineke.com**.

CHAPTER 6:
THE COST OF GETTING IT WRONG

When Spouses "Lawyer Up" Too Early

You may assume that the first thing to do when you're considering divorce is to "hire a lawyer". But when you or your spouse "lawyers up" at the start of a divorce in Florida, the process can become adversarial *very* quickly. An attorney may even advise you not to communicate with your spouse, warning that *"anything you say can be used against you in court"*.

While meant to protect clients legally, this advice can create additional tension, deepening misunderstandings, and making settlement and present and future cooperative parenting extremely difficult, if not impossible.

Pre-suit Divorce Mediation avoids these issues by providing a structured, neutral, confidential environment where both parties can openly discuss their needs and concerns. Sessions are scheduled in focused two-hour blocks, allowing meaningful progress without the adversarial back-and-forth of litigation. As a neutral mediator, I do not take sides or give legal advice. I do educate both spouses on Florida law; I assist with the couples understanding of their finances by preparing financial schedules and calculating child support; and I help design timesharing plans that work for the parents and their children.

In short, "lawyering up" too early often increases conflict, expense, and stress. Pre-Suit Mediation, on the other hand, fosters collaboration, preserves parenting relationships, and produces fair agreements that protect **both** of your long-term interests.

Why Peace Is So Hard After Court Filings Begin

The sad reality is that once a Florida divorce case has been filed, it can be difficult for couples to pause and choose to try to settle their disputes. An adversarial mindset develops quickly, causing you and your spouse to view one another as opponents rather than co-parents or partners in problem-solving, making compromise harder.

The procedural requirements of the court create pressure to meet deadlines, respond to motions, and adhere to formal schedules. This structure can make mediation and cooperation seem like a waste of time, rather than a simpler alternative.

And, once attorneys are involved, they'll likely focus on protecting their client's legal position rather than encouraging cooperation. Legal strategy often emphasizes negotiation from a position of strength, creating a confrontational mindset further reducing the capacity for compromise.

Meanwhile, the escalating legal costs of litigation can make you and your spouse feel invested in continuing court proceedings rather than stepping back and trying to work out a peaceable agreement. In essence, you may find yourself reasoning, *"I've spent this much time and money already, I might as well keep going"*, even though the emotional and financial toll is immense.

And after weeks and months of litigation, you and your spouse may feel hurt, frustrated, and even more distrustful. Emotions that have escalated in court can make it more psychologically challenging to return to a neutral, collaborative mindset.

Despite these challenges, introducing mediation early in a filed case can save time, reduce costs, and preserve relationships. As an attorney and a mediator, I help couples navigate mediation effectively, ensuring that agreements are fair, legally sound, and tailored to the family's unique circumstances.

Why Courtroom Wins Aren't Always Life Wins

In Florida divorce cases, winning in court doesn't always translate to a better life afterward. As I have often said (even as a litigator), ***"You don't win a divorce. You survive a divorce."***

The emotional toll, high costs, loss of control over your future, and damaged relationships caused by a courtroom divorce can be devastating. The turmoil is real, and I've witnessed it many times. When you head to court, you've missed out on creative solutions that could have made life far easier for you and your children.

Ultimately, surviving a divorce with a fair, practical, and enforceable agreement often matters more than "winning" in court. Rather than choosing to lawyer up, choosing pre-suit mediation with an experienced attorney-mediator like me helps couples achieve outcomes that truly support their long-term well-being.

PART IV:

Starting Your New Chapter With Closure, Confidence & Clarity

CHAPTER 7:
A BETTER KIND OF DIVORCE

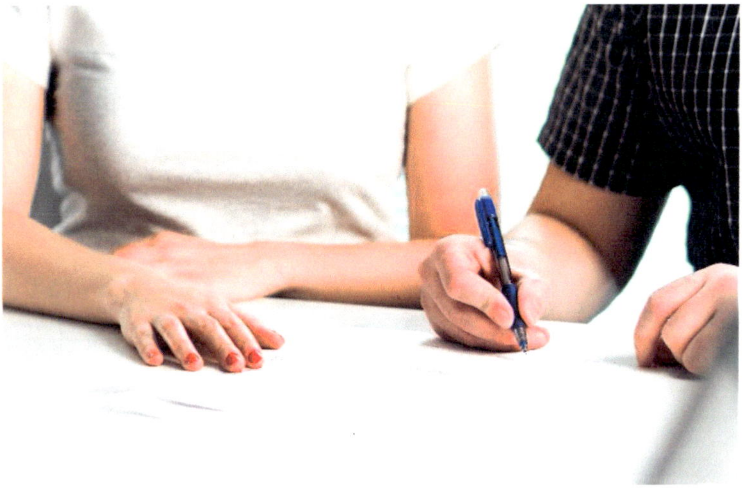

What Truly Successful Mediation Looks Like

In my eyes, truly successful mediation means that both you and your spouse have all the facts and are making informed choices between the various settlement options. More importantly, you both understand your rights and obligations under the terms of your negotiated contracts, and you are both satisfied with the result.

You may not have gotten everything you wanted (and you probably didn't), but at the end of the day, you know that you are going to be alright and that your children are going to be alright, too.

Build Parenting Plans That Work

I have over 30 years of experience working with families, both as a litigator and a mediator and my proprietary parenting plan reflects that experience. The best parenting plan is the one you throw in the drawer and never look at again. You and your co-parent work together cooperatively with the common goal of promoting the best interests of your children.

However, when communications break down and the parenting plan needs to come out to assist the parents in navigating a rocky place, the last thing they want is a cookie cutter form drafted by some AI Bot that fails to adequately address the issue at hand.

In my parenting plans, not only do I cover the basics, like timesharing schedules and shared parenting language, I have specific paragraphs drawn from real cases I personally handled that proactively address common areas of conflict, providing remedies when appropriate.

My goal is *always* to keep you out of court now and to keep you out of court in the future. A strong, custom drafted parenting plan will help accomplish just that.

How I Customize Your Marital Agreement

I have over 30 years of experience negotiating, drafting, and even challenging contracts like Marital Settlement Agreements. Having an experienced family law attorney like me draft your mediated divorce agreement is superior to using a generic online form.

As an attorney, I am able to tailor the written agreement to your unique financial and family circumstances—addressing complex asset division, business interests, retirement accounts, tax consequences, and debt allocation in ways a one-size-fits-all form cannot; I often anticipate and draft provisions for future contingencies (relocation, changes in income, modification of support, unforeseen health or education costs) to reduce later disputes; and I take steps to ensure legal enforceability and court compliance by using precise, jurisdiction-specific language and using terms that protect your rights while reducing the risk of costly litigation or voided provisions down the road.

Finding Peace Through Mediation

Heading into your divorce, you're not likely to be experiencing anything like peace, as everything can feel so out of control. But mediation puts control *back* into your hands. Information is power. During mediation, I supply the information, and you make the decisions.

My goal as your mediator is to help you and your spouse understand the law, and guide both of you toward resolutions that reduce stress, loss, and uncertainty. The process in itself can help make your divorce (and your future) far more stable, peaceable, and secure.

CHAPTER 8:
MEDIATION IN REAL LIFE

The Type Of Case That Sticks With Me

I was recently contacted by a couple who had been litigating their divorce for over two years and were getting nowhere. Their attorneys were hung up on the requirement for mandatory financial disclosure. Financial affidavits hadn't been started. There had been no financial schedules prepared, and there had been no discussions of settlement options with either client. The parties' case was just not going anywhere.

They had heard about pre-suit mediation from a friend and wanted to know if I could help. The divorce case had so polarized the couple that they didn't want to meet together. But after they spoke with their attorneys about mediating with me, we halted litigation (pending the outcome of mediation), rolled up our sleeves, and tackled the issues.

After a number of separate mediation sessions with each party, the case finally settled. I drafted the marital agreement for the attorneys to review with their clients. The clients signed a revised agreement that they were both satisfied with, and they were finally divorced within two to three weeks of signing.

That's the difference that an experienced, caring, and effective mediation attorney can make. This outcome would have been highly unlikely had the couple chosen to continue to litigate.

CHAPTER 9:
WHAT TO DO NEXT

How To Prepare For Mediation

To prepare for pre-suit mediation, be sure that your spouse is willing to mediate. You and the other party must both be willing to engage in meaningful and civil discussions about the relevant issues and make full and frank financial disclosures. While you don't have to be best friends, a shared commitment to the process is essential.

Once it has been determined that both of you

are willing to negotiate in good faith and work together, reach out to **Reineke Mediations**. Call **(813) 205-6675** or email me at **beth@bethreineke.com.**

Organize & Gather Financial Records: Once mediation has been scheduled, the next step is to gather key financial documents, such as detailed lists of your assets and liabilities. This may include:

- Your most current pay stubs
- Last year's W-2 forms
- Last year's tax returns
- Current bank statements
- Current financial statements
- Current loan statements

List Key Topics for Discussion: You may want to prepare a list of key topics you would like to discuss during mediation. This could include marital property, the division of retirement benefits, child support and alimony, timesharing schedules, parenting concerns, guidelines for future communications, and any other issues unique to your family or situation.

Establish Your Priorities: Finally, determine what is truly important to you, what terms you are willing to negotiate, and what is non-negotiable. At the same time, understand that mediation involves compromise, and you may not get everything you want.

Be Realistic About Time Frames: Pre-suit Mediation is typically faster than litigation, but it still requires time. After reaching an agreement, it takes time to draft, review, sign, and file the necessary documents with the court. The entire process can take approximately 2 to 3 months from start to finish. Contested litigation, by contrast, can take a year or more, not including potential post-judgment appeals.

Understand The Costs of Mediation & The Financial Benefits: Pre-Suit Divorce is significantly less expensive than a contested divorce. According to USA Today, the average cost of a mildly contested divorce in the United States without children is $13,500 and $20,300 with children. My mediation process is significantly less expensive. Sessions are booked in two-hour blocks of time, and you pay at the end of each session. A retainer is only taken when a settlement has been reached. The total cost of mediation is a fraction of the cost of contested divorce litigation, involving two competing attorneys.

Drafting Agreements (Contracts): At the conclusion of your mediation sessions, I will draft your contracts and court documents for your uncontested divorce. You will have the opportunity to review all documents before signing, and I'll provide you with instructions on filing them with the court and scheduling your final hearing.

All of this preparation can help save you and your spouse considerable time, reduce costs, and make you feel more in control of your future and the outcome of your divorce.

The "Golden Rule" For Those Trying To Choose Peace Over Battle

When choosing mediation, above all, be patient with the other party if they are not as prepared as you are for mediation and are not ready to settle at first.

Trust that your mediator is going to get the other party up to speed and that, if both of you are committed to not litigating, an agreement *will* be reached.

PART V:
FINAL THOUGHTS

CHAPTER 10:

A NOTE TO YOU FROM ATTORNEY-MEDIATOR BETH REINEKE

Divorce doesn't have to be a war, and the next steps forward don't have to ruin your health, finances, or waste your time.

If you and your spouse are ready to move forward with an uncontested divorce, reach out to **Reineke Mediations** today. I'm here to help spare you the added expense, turmoil, and uncertainty of a contested divorce. I'll help put you back in the driver's seat and empower both of you to move on with greater certainty, clarity, and an agreement that will work.

Before you call a lawyer, before you download a vague online form, and before you share your thoughts with ChatGPT, **give me a call**.

I'll provide you with the professional, tailored, legally binding solutions that both of you need to part ways amicably, fairly, and on the best foot possible.

Ready to Get Started? We're Ready to Help.

Reineke Mediations

(813) 205-6675

https://www.bethreineke.com/

Book Your Mediation Session Today

Notes

Made in the USA
Monee, IL
05 November 2026

67387951R00048